FAVORITE BRAND NAME

Celebrate

with KRAFT® Cool Whip®

Publications International, Ltd.

Senior Brand Manager: Lisa Coker
Assistant Brand Manager: Kristen Walsh
Kraft Kitchens Division Manager: Debra-Ann Robinson
Kraft Kitchens Consumer Foods Associate: Normajean Longfield
Kraft Kitchens Senior Technician: Donna Mangilit

Photography: Kraft Creative Services
Photographers: Allen Owens, Louis Wallach
Photographers' Assistant: Sean Burns
Food Stylists: Leslie Medina-Scocca, Cathy Paukner
Assistant Food Stylist: Erna Krueger
Prop Stylist: Heather Bean
Prop Assistant: Rita Neiman
Photo Coordinator: Gail Manno

Pictured on the front cover: Chocolate Ribbon Pie *(page 11)*.

Pictured on the back cover *(clockwise from top):* Toffee Bar Dessert *(page 54)*,
Cool Bananas *(page 48)* and Holiday Chocolate Berry Trifle *(page 16)*.

ISBN: 0-7853-3589-7

Manufactured in China.

8 7 6 5 4 3 2 1

Microwave Cooking: Microwave ovens vary in wattage. The microwave times
given in this publication are approximate. Use the cooking times as guidelines and
check for doneness before adding more time. Consult manufacturer's instructions
for suitable micro-safe cooking dishes.

Preparation: Preparation times are based on the approximate amount of time
required to assemble the recipe before cooking, baking, chilling or serving. These
times include preparation steps such as measuring, chopping and mixing. The fact
that some preparation and cooking can be done simultaneously is taken into
account. Preparation times of optional ingredients and serving suggestions are not
included.

Contents

Make every day a day to remember. With COOL WHIP Whipped Topping, whether you are looking for a tasty tidbit or a divine dessert, the perfect recipe for all your celebrations is just around the corner. From classic holiday recipes to everyday snacking ideas, you'll discover that COOL WHIP is more than just a topping.

In our efforts to help make all your desserts special, we compiled 75 new and classic recipes created just to your liking. These spectacular treats are simple to make and take 30 minutes or less (and in some instances, 5 minutes or less) to prepare. So, stop racking your brain looking for the ultimate goody. Let your fingers do the walking through this fabulous cookbook and come *Celebrate with COOL WHIP*— moments of sweet surprises and sudden smiles are just around the corner for all your life's occasions!

How much COOL WHIP to use:

COOL WHIP Whipped Topping comes in 3 sizes. To estimate recipe needs, the number of cups per tub is listed in the chart below.

	Cool Whip Regular	Cool Whip Extra Creamy	Cool Whip Lite/Free
TUB SIZE	AMOUNT	AMOUNT	AMOUNT
8 ounces	3½ cups	3 cups	3¼ cups
12 ounces	5¼ cups	4½ cups	5 cups
16 ounces	7 cups	– – –	6½ cups*

COOL WHIP Free is not available in a 16 ounce tub.

How To Thaw COOL WHIP

Place tub of COOL WHIP Whipped Topping, unopened, in the refrigerator. For complete thawing, allow these times:

• 4 hours for 8-ounce tub

• 5 hours for 12-ounce tub

• 6 hours for 16-ounce tub

Do not thaw COOL WHIP in the microwave.

How to Store COOL WHIP

- For long-term storage, keep COOL WHIP Whipped Topping in the freezer.

- Once thawed, refrigerate for no more than 2 weeks, or re-freeze.

- Don't let the container stand in a hot kitchen—the topping will soften and begin to liquify.

- Desserts prepared with COOL WHIP Whipped Topping should be stored in the refrigerator or freezer.

How to Use COOL WHIP

- COOL WHIP Regular, Extra Creamy and COOL WHIP Lite Whipped Toppings can usually be used interchangeably in recipes. When used with gelatin or high-acid fruits, COOL WHIP Lite may produce a softer set.

- COOL WHIP Free is not interchangeable with all the recipes in this magazine. When substituting COOL WHIP Free, the end result will be a very soft set and slightly lower volume.

- Drain thawed frozen fruit before serving with COOL WHIP. The juice may make the topping appear curdled.

- COOL WHIP Whipped Topping can be substituted for an equal amount of whipped cream. If the recipe calls for liquid cream to be whipped, simply double the amount of liquid cream called for and substitute that amount of COOL WHIP®.

- Thaw COOL WHIP Whipped Topping completely before measuring or stirring into ingredients.

- COOL WHIP Whipped Topping can be scooped like ice cream directly from the tub while still frozen.

- Completely thawed COOL WHIP Whipped Topping can be spooned into a pastry bag or decorating tube and piped decoratively like whipped cream or frosting.

For a big reason, little reason or no reason at all, get together with a COOL WHIP dessert today!

![Kraft Cool Whip logo]

HOLIDAY CLASSICS

'Tis the season, so there is always a reason to celebrate. A sampling of rich and creamy Fluffy Cherry Cheesecake, classic Chocolate Ribbon Pie and refreshing Cranberry Mousse Mold are palate pleasers everyone will enjoy. Make the most of all your holiday gatherings and serve luscious COOL WHIP treats!

Fluffy Cherry Cheesecake
(page 10)

Fluffy Cheesecake

Prep: 15 minutes

1 package (8 ounces)
   PHILADELPHIA Cream
   Cheese, softened
⅓ cup sugar
1 tub (8 ounces) COOL
   WHIP Whipped
   Topping, thawed

1 prepared graham
   cracker crumb crust
   (6 ounces or 9 inches)

BEAT cream cheese and sugar in large bowl with wire whisk or electric mixer on high speed until smooth. Gently stir in whipped topping. Spoon into crust.

REFRIGERATE 3 hours or until set. Garnish as desired.

Makes 8 servings

Fluffy Cherry Cheesecake: Prepare and refrigerate as directed above. Spoon 1½ cups cherry pie filling over top of pie.

Fluffy Cranberry Cheesecake: Beat in 1 cup whole berry cranberry sauce with cream cheese. Proceed as directed above.

Fluffy Pumpkin Cheesecake: Increase sugar to ½ cup. Beat in 1 cup canned pumpkin and ½ teaspoon pumpkin pie spice with cream cheese. Proceed as directed above.

Fluffy Caramel Pecan Cheesecake: Beat cream cheese and sugar in large bowl with wire whisk until smooth. Gently stir in whipped topping. Spoon 1 cup cream cheese mixture into crust; spread evenly. Top with ⅓ cup KRAFT Caramel Topping and ¼ cup toasted pecans; spread evenly. Top with remaining cream cheese mixture. Refrigerate 3 hours or until set. Garnish with additional caramel topping, whipped topping and pecans.

Chocolate Ribbon Pie

Prep: 15 minutes

4 ounces PHILADELPHIA
  Cream Cheese,
  softened
2 tablespoons sugar
1 tablespoon milk
1 tub (8 ounces) COOL
  WHIP Whipped
  Topping, thawed

1 prepared chocolate
  flavor crumb crust
  (6 ounces or 9 inches)
2 cups cold milk
2 packages (4-serving size
  each) JELL-O
  Chocolate Flavor
  Instant Pudding & Pie
  Filling

BEAT cream cheese, sugar and 1 tablespoon milk in large bowl until smooth. Gently stir in half of the whipped topping. Spread over crust.

POUR 2 cups milk into large bowl. Add pudding mixes. Beat with wire whisk 2 minutes (mixture will be thick). Pour over cream cheese layer.

REFRIGERATE 4 hours or until set. Just before serving, spread or dollop remaining whipped topping over pudding layer. Garnish with shaved chocolate.   *Makes 8 servings*

KRAFT

Cool Whip
Fun Fact

The top 3 scoring recipes are: Strawberry Shortcut (p.67), Pudding in a Cloud (p.38) and Fluffy Cheesecake (p.10).

Holiday Dessert Mold

Prep: 15 minutes

1 package (12 ounces)
    marble pound cake,
    cut into 12 slices
3 cups cold milk
1 package (4-serving size)
    JELL-O Vanilla <u>or</u>
    White Chocolate
    Flavor Instant Pudding
    & Pie Filling
1 tub (8 ounces) COOL
    WHIP Whipped
    Topping, thawed

1 package (4-serving size)
    JELL-O Lemon Flavor
    Instant Pudding & Pie
    Filling
2 squares BAKER'S Semi-
    Sweet Baking
    Chocolate, melted
    (optional)

CUT cake slices in half to form triangles. Arrange cake triangles in bottom and up side of 9- or 10-inch springform pan.

POUR 1½ cups milk into large bowl. Add vanilla pudding mix. Beat with wire whisk 1 minute. Gently stir in half of the whipped topping. Spoon pudding mixture over cake in pan.

POUR remaining milk into large bowl. Add lemon pudding mix. Beat with wire whisk 1 minute. Gently stir in remaining whipped topping. Spoon pudding mixture over pudding in pan. Drizzle with chocolate.

REFRIGERATE 4 hours or overnight.   *Makes 10 servings*

Note: A foil-lined 9- or 10-inch round cake pan can be substituted for the springform pan. DO NOT cut cake slices into triangles. Place 7 whole cake slices lengthwise around side of pan; cut remaining 5 slices to fit in bottom. Proceed as directed above.

Holiday Dessert Mold

Double Berry Cake Squares

Prep: 10 minutes

1 package (12 ounces)
    pound cake, cut into
    10 slices
3 tablespoons cranberry
    juice cocktail
2 packages (10 to
    12 ounces each)
    frozen raspberries

2 tablespoons sugar
2½ cups cold milk
2 packages (4-serving size
    each) JELL-O Vanilla
    Flavor Instant Pudding
1 tub (8 ounces) COOL
    WHIP Whipped
    Topping, thawed

ARRANGE cake slices in bottom of 13×9-inch pan. Drizzle with cranberry juice. Top with frozen raspberries, separating raspberries as needed. Sprinkle with sugar.

POUR milk into large bowl. Add pudding mixes. Beat with wire whisk 1 minute. Gently stir in 1 cup whipped topping. Spoon mixture over raspberries in pan. Top with remaining whipped topping.

REFRIGERATE until ready to serve or overnight. Garnish as desired. *Makes 15 servings*

Mother's Little Angel Cake

Prep: 15 minutes

1 angel food cake
    (10-inch)
1 tub (8 ounces) COOL
    WHIP Whipped
    Topping, thawed

1 cup halved strawberries

PLACE cake on serving plate. Frost top and sides of cake with whipped topping; decorate with strawberries. Refrigerate until ready to serve. *Makes 10 servings*

Double Berry Cake Squares

Holiday Chocolate Berry Trifle

Prep: 15 minutes

3 cups cold milk
2 packages (4-serving size
    each) JELL-O
    Chocolate Flavor
    Instant Pudding & Pie
    Filling
1 tub (12 ounces) COOL
    WHIP Whipped
    Topping, thawed

1 baked 9-inch square
    brownie layer, cut into
    1-inch cubes
1 pint raspberries

POUR cold milk into large bowl. Add pudding mixes. Beat with wire whisk 2 minutes. Gently stir in 2 cups whipped topping.

PLACE half of the brownie cubes in 2-quart serving bowl. Top with half of the pudding mixture, half of the raspberries and 2 cups whipped topping. Repeat layers. Top with remaining whipped topping.

REFRIGERATE 1 hour or until ready to serve.

Makes 12 servings

KRAFT
Cool Whip.
Fun Fact

As a topping, COOL WHIP is most often used on cakes, pies, JELL-O and fruit.

Holiday Chocolate Berry Trifle

Double Layer Pumpkin Pie

Prep: 15 minutes

4 ounces PHILADELPHIA
Cream Cheese,
softened
1 tablespoon milk
1 tablespoon sugar
1 tub (8 ounces) COOL
WHIP Whipped
Topping, thawed
1 prepared graham
cracker crumb crust
(6 ounces <u>or</u> 9 inches)

1 cup cold milk
1 can (16 ounces)
pumpkin
2 packages (4-serving size
each) JELL-O Vanilla
Flavor Instant Pudding
& Pie Filling
1 teaspoon ground
cinnamon
½ teaspoon ground ginger
¼ teaspoon ground cloves

MIX cream cheese, 1 tablespoon milk and sugar in large bowl with wire whisk until smooth. Gently stir in 1½ cups whipped topping. Spread onto bottom of crust.

POUR 1 cup milk into large bowl. Add pumpkin, pudding mixes, cinnamon, ginger and cloves. Beat with wire whisk until well mixed (mixture will be thick). Spread over cream cheese layer.

REFRIGERATE 4 hours or until set. Garnish with remaining whipped topping. *Makes 8 servings*

Helpful Hint: Soften cream cheese in microwave on HIGH 15 to 20 seconds.

Easy COOL WHIP® Frosting

Prep: 10 minutes

1 cup cold milk
1 package (4-serving size)
    JELL-O Instant
    Pudding & Pie Filling,
    any flavor

¼ cup powdered sugar
    (optional)
1 tub (8 ounces) COOL
    WHIP Whipped
    Topping, thawed

POUR milk into medium bowl. Add pudding mix and sugar.

BEAT with wire whisk 2 minutes. Gently stir in whipped topping.

SPREAD on cake immediately.

*Makes about 4 cups or enough to fill and
frost 2 (9-inch) cake layers*

Easy Festive Frosting: Prepare as directed above using
JELL-O Vanilla Flavor Instant Pudding & Pie Filling. Add
1 tablespoon grated orange peel, ½ teaspoon ground
cinnamon and ¼ teaspoon ground nutmeg with pudding mix.

Easy Mocha Frosting: Substitute ½ cup chilled strongly
brewed MAXWELL HOUSE Coffee and ½ cup cold milk for
1 cup milk. Use JELL-O Chocolate or Vanilla Flavor Instant
Pudding & Pie Filling.

Creamy Pumpkin Bars

Tired of boring pumpkin pie? Try these great pumpkin spiced bars for a new twist on the traditional holiday dessert.

Prep: 20 minutes

1½ cups graham cracker crumbs
⅔ cup chopped walnuts, toasted
½ cup (1 stick) butter *or* margarine, melted
¼ cup sugar
1 package (8 ounces) PHILADELPHIA Cream Cheese, softened
2 cups cold milk

2 packages (4-serving size each) JELL-O Vanilla Flavor Instant Pudding & Pie Filling
1 can (16 ounces) pumpkin
2 teaspoons pumpkin pie spice
1 tub (8 ounces) COOL WHIP Whipped Topping, thawed
Ground nutmeg (optional)

MIX graham cracker crumbs, ⅓ cup walnuts, butter and sugar in 13×9-inch pan. Press firmly onto bottom of pan. Refrigerate until ready to fill.

BEAT cream cheese in large bowl with electric mixer on low speed until smooth. Gradually add ½ cup milk. Add remaining milk, pudding mixes, pumpkin and spice. Beat on low speed about 2 minutes or until well blended. Stir in half of the whipped topping. Pour over crust. Dollop or spread remaining whipped topping over pudding mixture.

REFRIGERATE 2 hours or until set. Sprinkle with remaining walnuts or nutmeg. Garnish as desired.   *Makes 15 servings*

Creamy Pumpkin Bars

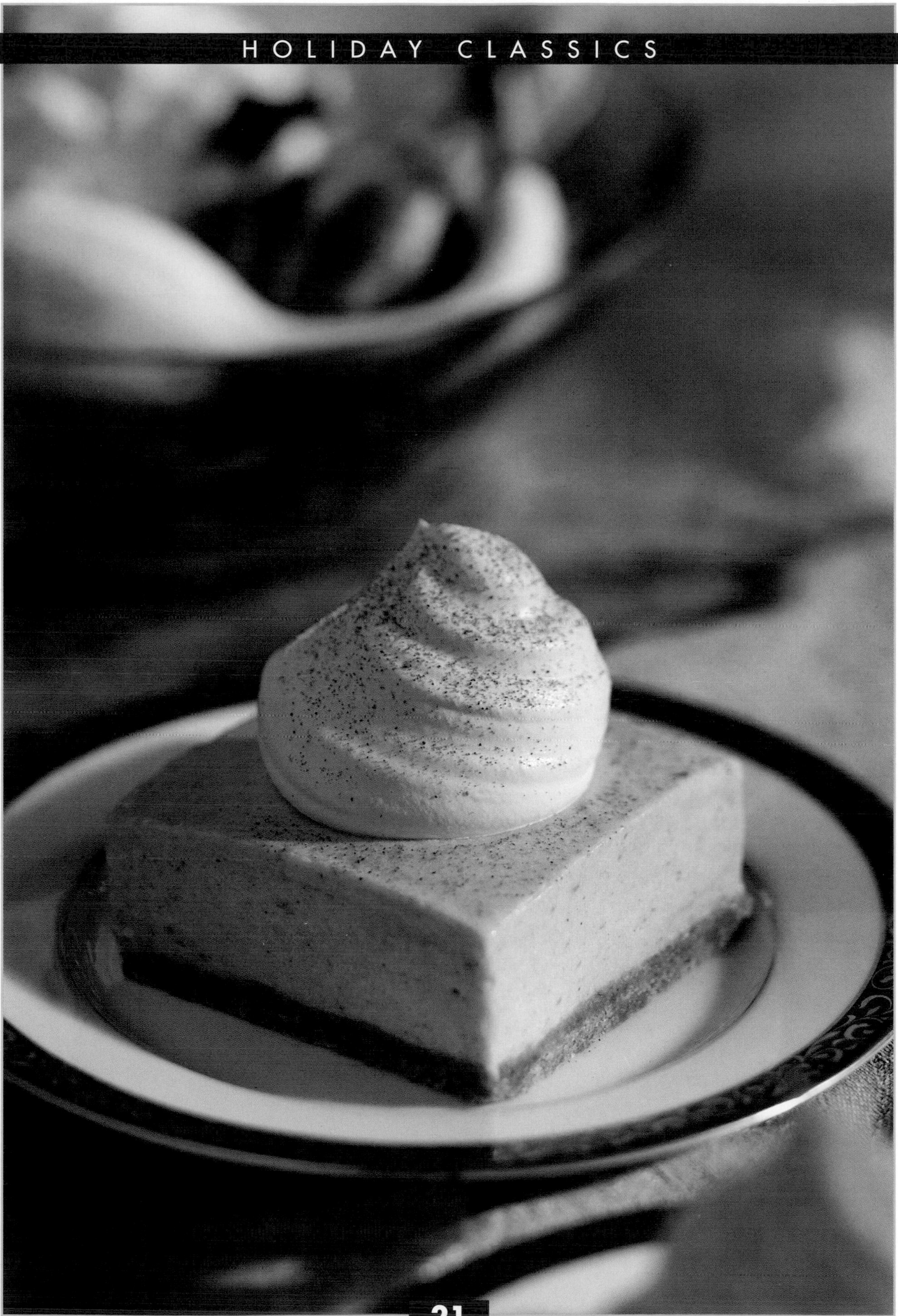

Cranberry Mousse Mold

Prep: 30 minutes

1½ cups boiling water
1 package (8-serving size)
  or 2 packages
  (4-serving size each)
  JELL-O Brand
  Cranberry Flavor
  Gelatin Dessert

1 cup cold water
1 can (16 ounces) whole
  berry cranberry sauce
1 tub (8 ounces) COOL
  WHIP Whipped
  Topping, thawed

STIR boiling water into gelatin in large bowl 2 minutes or until completely dissolved. Stir in cold water and cranberry sauce. Spoon 2 cups gelatin mixture into 6-cup mold. Refrigerate about 30 minutes or until set but not firm (should stick to finger and mound).

MEANWHILE, refrigerate remaining gelatin mixture about 30 minutes or until slightly thickened (consistency of unbeaten egg whites).

STIR in 2 cups whipped topping with wire whisk until smooth. Pour over gelatin layer in mold.

REFRIGERATE 4 hours or until firm. Unmold. Garnish with remaining whipped topping.   *Makes 12 servings*

Unmolding: Dip mold in warm water for about 15 seconds. Gently pull gelatin from around edges with moist fingers. Place moistened serving plate on top of mold. Invert mold and plate; holding mold and plate together, shake slightly to loosen. Gently remove mold and center gelatin on plate.

Cranberry Mousse Mold

COOL WHIP

SWEETIE PIES

If you think pie making takes lots of time and energy, then check out this dynamite chapter. Add pizzazz to your dinner table with a delectable slice of homemade Fudge Brownie Pie or Key Lime Pie. Whether you are looking for something for a fabulous feast or a simple patio party, look no further. With COOL WHIP, perfect pies are just moments away.

Fudge Brownie Pie (page 26)

Fudge Brownie Pie

The fabulous combination of a rich and chewy fudge brownie, and smooth and creamy chocolate pudding is the perfect taste sensation to get your taste buds jumping.

Prep: 20 minutes

1 package (19 to 21 ounces) fudge brownie mix
1 cup cold milk
1 package (4-serving size) JELL-O Chocolate Flavor Instant Pudding & Pie Filling

1 tub (8 ounces) COOL WHIP Whipped Topping, thawed

PREPARE brownie mix as directed on package. Bake in greased 9-inch pie plate 40 minutes or until done according to doneness test on brownie package. Cool completely on wire rack.

SCOOP out center of brownie, using spoon, leaving 1-inch crust around edge and thin layer of brownie on bottom; reserve brownie scraps.

POUR milk into medium bowl. Add pudding mix. Beat with wire whisk until blended. Gently stir in half of the whipped topping and all but ¼ cup reserved brownie scraps. Spoon into center of crust. Top with remaining whipped topping and reserved ¼ cup brownie scraps.

REFRIGERATE 3 hours or until ready to serve. Garnish as desired. *Makes 8 servings*

Raspberry Cream Pie

Prep: 10 minutes

1 package (8 ounces)
  PHILADELPHIA Cream
  Cheese, softened
¾ cup raspberry fruit
  spread
⅓ cup cold milk
1 package (4-serving size)
  JELL-O Vanilla Flavor
  Instant Pudding & Pie
  Filling

1 tub (8 ounces) COOL
  WHIP Whipped
  Topping, thawed
Red liquid food coloring
  (8 to 10 drops)
1 prepared chocolate
  flavor crumb crust
  (6 ounces or 9 inches)

BEAT cream cheese and fruit spread in large bowl with wire whisk until smooth. Gradually beat in milk until smooth. Add pudding mix. Beat 2 minutes. Reserve ½ cup whipped topping. Gently stir remaining whipped topping into pudding mixture. Stir in food coloring until desired color is achieved. Spoon into crust.

REFRIGERATE 3 hours. Garnish with remaining whipped topping.   *Makes 8 servings*

Fluffy Lemon Fruit Pie

Prep: 10 minutes

1 can (21 ounces) cherry
pie filling
1 prepared graham
cracker crumb crust
(6 ounces or 9 inches)
1 package (8 ounces)
PHILADELPHIA Cream
Cheese, softened

1 cup cold milk
1 package (4-serving size)
JELL-O Lemon Flavor
Instant Pudding & Pie
Filling
1 tub (8 ounces) COOL
WHIP Whipped
Topping, thawed

SPREAD half of the cherry pie filling on bottom of crust.

BEAT cream cheese in large bowl with wire whisk until smooth.
Gradually beat in milk until well blended. Add pudding mix.
Beat until smooth. Gently stir in half of the whipped topping.
Spread over pie filling.

SPREAD remaining whipped topping over pudding mixture.
Spoon remaining cherry pie filling over whipped topping layer.

REFRIGERATE 3 hours or until set. Garnish as desired.

Makes 8 servings

KRAFT
Cool Whip
Fun Fact

COOL WHIP was
introduced in 1967 and
in 1997 celebrated its
30th Anniversary!

Fluffy Lemon Fruit Pie

Key Lime Pie

Add some zing to the end of your meal with the zesty lime flavor and cool, creamy texture of this fabulous pie.

Prep: 15 minutes

1 cup boiling water
1 package (4-serving size) JELL-O Brand Lime Flavor Gelatin Dessert
1 can (14 ounces) sweetened condensed milk
½ cup lime juice

1 to 2 teaspoon grated lime peel
1 tub (8 ounces) COOL WHIP Whipped Topping, thawed
1 prepared graham cracker crumb crust (6 ounces <u>or</u> 9 inches)
Lime slices (optional)

STIR boiling water into gelatin in large bowl 2 minutes or until completely dissolved. Stir in condensed milk, lime juice and lime peel. Refrigerate about 30 minutes or until slightly thickened (consistency of unbeaten egg whites).

RESERVE ½ cup whipped topping. Gently stir remaining whipped topping into gelatin mixture. Spoon into pie crust.

REFRIGERATE 3 hours or until firm. Garnish with reserved whipped topping and lime slices.   *Makes 8 servings*

Key Lime Pie

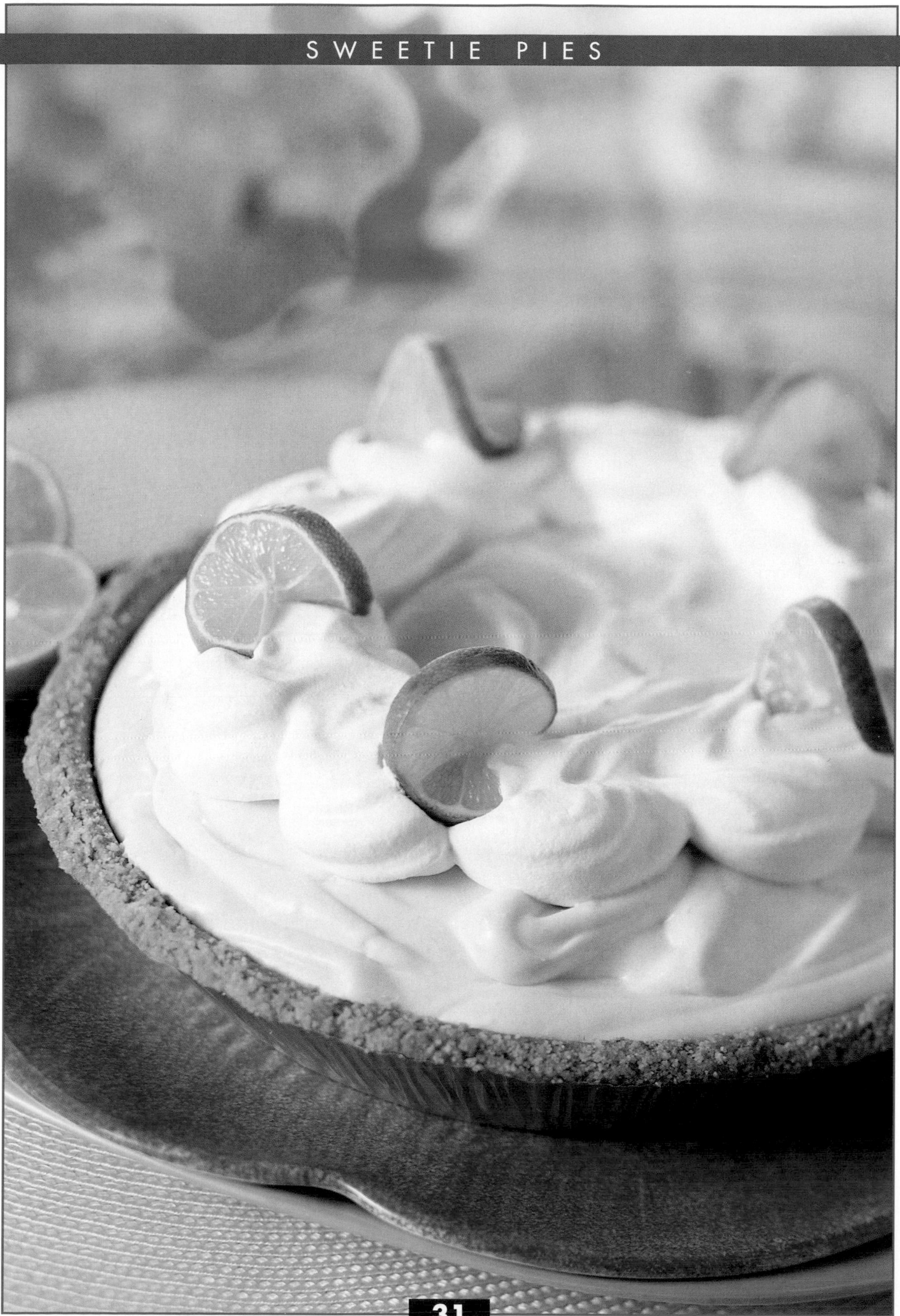

Italian Cheese Pie

Prep: 10 minutes

1 cup ricotta cheese
¾ cup cold milk
1½ teaspoons grated
    orange peel
1 package (4-serving size)
    JELL-O White
    Chocolate or Vanilla
    Flavor Instant Pudding
    & Pie Filling

1 tub (8 ounces) COOL
    WHIP Whipped
    Topping, thawed
½ cup plus 2 tablespoons
    BAKER'S Semi-Sweet
    Real Chocolate Chips
1 prepared shortbread
    crumb crust (6 ounces
    or 9 inches)
Orange slices

BEAT ricotta cheese, milk and orange peel in large bowl with wire whisk until blended. Add pudding mix. Beat with wire whisk 1 to 2 minutes. Gently stir in 2 cups whipped topping and ½ cup chocolate chips. Spoon into crust.

REFRIGERATE 2 hours or until firm. Garnish with remaining whipped topping, remaining 2 tablespoons chocolate chips and orange slices.   *Makes 8 servings*

Triple Layer Chocolate Pie

Prep: 15 minutes

2 cups cold milk
2 packages (4-serving size
    each) JELL-O
    Chocolate Flavor
    Instant Pudding & Pie
    Filling

1 prepared chocolate
    flavor crumb crust
    (6 ounces or 9 inches)
1 tub (8 ounces) COOL
    WHIP Whipped
    Topping, thawed

POUR milk into large bowl. Add pudding mixes. Beat with wire whisk until blended. Spoon 1½ cups pudding into bottom of crust.

GENTLY stir half of the whipped topping into remaining pudding. Spread over pudding in crust. Top with remaining whipped topping.

REFRIGERATE 3 hours or until set. Garnish as desired.

Makes 8 servings

GERMAN'S® Sweet Chocolate Pie

Prep: 10 minutes

1 package (4 ounces) BAKER'S GERMAN'S Sweet Baking Chocolate or 3 squares BAKER'S Semi-Sweet Baking Chocolate
⅓ cup milk
4 ounces PHILADELPHIA Cream Cheese, softened

2 tablespoons sugar
1 tub (8 ounces) COOL WHIP Whipped Topping, thawed
1 baked pastry shell (8- or 9-inch) cooled or 1 prepared graham cracker crumb crust (6 ounces or 9 inches)

MICROWAVE chocolate and 2 tablespoons milk in large microwavable bowl on HIGH 1½ to 2 minutes or until chocolate is almost melted, stirring halfway through heating time. Stir until chocolate is completely melted.

BEAT in cream cheese, sugar and remaining milk with wire whisk until well blended. Refrigerate about 10 minutes to cool. Gently stir in whipped topping until smooth. Spoon into crust.

FREEZE 4 hours or overnight. Garnish with additional whipped topping and chocolate curls, if desired. Let stand at room temperature or in refrigerator about 15 minutes or until pie can be cut easily.

Makes 8 servings

Banana Caramel Café Pie

Prep: 10 minutes

1 large ripe banana,
   sliced
1 prepared chocolate
   flavor crumb crust
   (6 ounces or 9 inches)
2 cups cold milk
1 to 2 tablespoons
   MAXWELL HOUSE
   Instant Coffee

2 packages (4-serving size
   each) JELL-O White
   Chocolate or Vanilla
   Flavor Instant Pudding
   & Pie Filling
1 tub (8 ounces) COOL
   WHIP Whipped
   Topping, thawed
¼ cup KRAFT Caramel
   Topping

PLACE banana slices on bottom of crust.

POUR milk and coffee granules into medium bowl; stir 1 minute. Add pudding mixes. Beat with wire whisk 1 minute (mixture will be thick). Gently stir in half of the whipped topping.

SPOON pudding mixture into crust. Refrigerate 3 hours.

SPOON some caramel topping onto 8 dessert plates; top each with a slice of pie. Top with remaining whipped topping. Just before serving, garnish with caramel topping as desired.

Makes 8 servings

KRAFT
Cool Whip
Fun Fact
The top 3 cities that consume the most COOL WHIP per capita are: Minneapolis, Salt Lake City/Boise and Syracuse.

Banana Caramel Café Pie

SNACKS IN A SNAP

Bring the kid out in everyone with the magic of COOL WHIP. Fruit in a Cloud, Cookie Cones and Crazy Mixed-Up Bars are just some of the snackin' sensations that will hold everyone over until the next meal. It takes only moments to whip it up with COOL WHIP!

Fruit in a Cloud (page 38)

Fruit in a Cloud

Prep: 10 minutes

1 tub (8 ounces) COOL
WHIP Whipped
Topping, thawed

3 cups assorted fresh fruit,
such as blueberries,
grapes, sliced kiwi,
melon, peaches and
strawberries

SPOON whipped topping evenly into 10 dessert dishes. Using back of spoon, make depression in center; spread whipped topping up side of each dish. Refrigerate until ready to serve.

SPOON fruit into center of whipped topping just before serving.

Makes 10 servings

Pudding in a Cloud: Spoon 2 cups thawed COOL WHIP Whipped Topping into 6 dessert dishes as directed above. Pour 2 cups cold milk into medium bowl. Add 1 package (4-serving size) JELL-O Instant Pudding & Pie Filling, any flavor. Beat with wire whisk 2 minutes. Spoon pudding into center of whipped topping. Refrigerate until ready to serve. Makes 6 servings.

Cool Cappuccino Shake

Prep: 5 minutes

1 cup milk
1 envelope MAXWELL
HOUSE Cappuccino,
any flavor

½ cup COOL WHIP
Whipped Topping,
frozen

PLACE milk and cappuccino in blender container; cover. Blend on high speed until cappuccino is dissolved. Add whipped topping; cover. Blend until smooth. Serve at once with additional whipped topping, if desired. Garnish as desired.

Makes 1 serving

S'Mores

Prep: 15 minutes

10 whole graham crackers, broken in half

5 bars (1.55 ounces each) milk chocolate candy, broken into quarters

1 jar (7½ ounces) marshmallow creme

1 tub (8 ounces) COOL WHIP Whipped Topping, thawed

TOP graham cracker halves with chocolate bar quarters.

REMOVE lid from marshmallow creme. Microwave marshmallow creme on MEDIUM 40 seconds. Spoon into large bowl. Gently stir in whipped topping until well mixed.

SPOON marshmallow mixture on top of chocolate.

Makes 20 servings

Ice Cream Sundaes

Prep: 10 minutes

1 pint (2 cups) ice cream, any flavor

½ cup dessert topping, any flavor

2 cups thawed COOL WHIP Whipped Topping

Maraschino cherries (optional)

SCOOP ice cream into 4 dessert or sundae dishes. Drizzle topping over ice cream. Dollop with whipped topping. Garnish with cherries. Serve immediately.

Makes 4 servings

Cool Whip (KRAFT) Fun Fact

More than 6 out of 10 consumers reuse COOL WHIP tubs for leftovers and collectibles.

Crazy Mixed-Up Bars

Prep: 10 minutes

1 package (10 ounces) marshmallows
4 squares BAKER'S Semi-Sweet Baking Chocolate, chopped

1 tub (8 ounces) COOL WHIP Whipped Topping, thawed
1 package (13 ounces) POST Cocoa or Fruity PEBBLES Cereal

MICROWAVE marshmallows in large microwavable bowl on HIGH 1½ minutes until melted. Beat with wire whisk until smooth. Stir in chocolate until melted. Stir in whipped topping. Stir in cereal until well blended.

SPREAD mixture into foil-lined 13×9-inch pan sprayed with no-stick cooking spray. Freeze 4 hours or overnight.

Makes 20 bars

Fruity Mixed-Up Bars: Substitute 4 squares BAKER'S White Chocolate Baking Squares for semi-sweet baking chocolate and Fruity PEBBLES Cereal for Cocoa PEBBLES; proceed as directed above.

Cookies and Creme Snacks

Prep: 5 minutes

1 cup chocolate sandwich cookie crumbs or chocolate wafer cookie crumbs

1 tub (8 ounces) COOL WHIP Whipped Topping, thawed

STIR cookie crumbs into whipped topping. Spoon into snack cups or flat-bottom ice cream cones.

REFRIGERATE or freeze until ready to serve.

Makes 6 to 8 servings

Fruity Mixed-Up Bars and Crazy Mixed-Up Bars

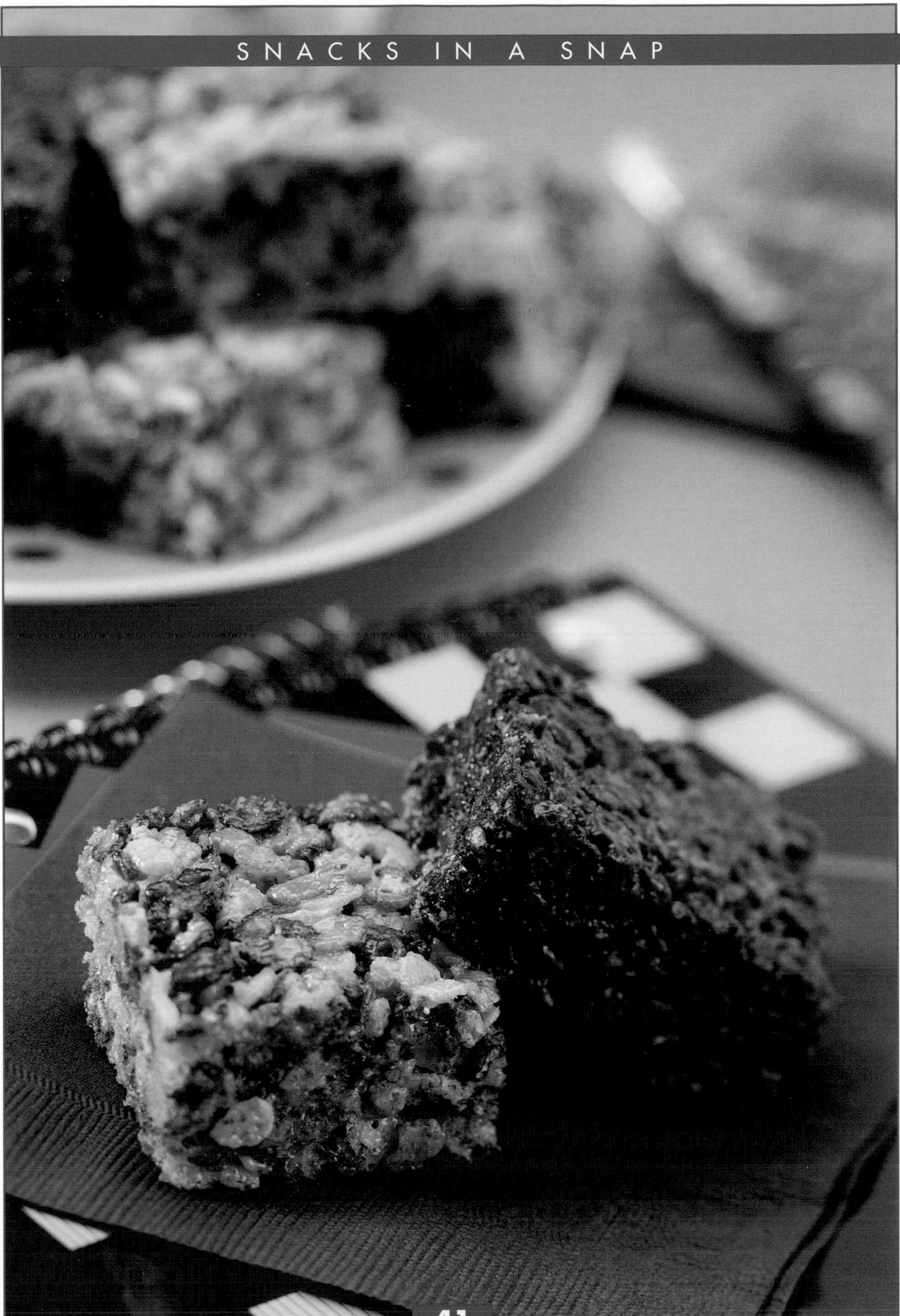

COOL WHIP® Smoothie

Prep: 1 minute

1 container (8 ounces) BREYERS Vanilla or Strawberry Lowfat Yogurt

1 cup thawed COOL WHIP Whipped Topping
1 cup chopped strawberries (optional)

PLACE yogurt, whipped topping and strawberries in blender container; cover. Blend until smooth. Garnish with additional whipped topping, if desired. Serve immediately.

Makes 2 servings

Southern Ambrosia

Prep: 15 minutes

3 cups fresh pineapple chunks
2 bananas, sliced
3 cans (15 ounces each) mandarin orange segments, drained
1 jar (6 ounces) maraschino cherries, drained

½ cup coarsely chopped pecans, toasted
1¼ cups BAKER'S ANGEL FLAKE Coconut
1 tub (8 ounces) COOL WHIP Whipped Topping, thawed

LAYER half of the pineapple, bananas, oranges, cherries and pecans in straight-sided glass bowl. Sprinkle with half of the coconut. Repeat layers.

TOP with whipped topping, spreading to edges of bowl to seal. Decorate with additional maraschino cherries, pecan halves and toasted coconut.

REFRIGERATE until ready to serve.

Makes 6 cups

COOL WHIP® Smoothie

Dirt Cups

Dirt Cups and Sand Cups can also be served frozen. Prepare as directed. Freeze 3 hours or overnight.

Prep: 15 minutes

1 package (16 ounces) chocolate sandwich cookies
2 cups cold milk
1 package (4-serving size) JELL-O Chocolate Flavor Instant Pudding & Pie Filling
1 tub (8 ounces) COOL WHIP Whipped Topping, thawed

8 to 10 (7-ounce) paper or plastic cups
Suggested garnishes: gummy worms or other gummy candies, candy flowers, chopped peanuts, granola

CRUSH cookies in zipper-style plastic bag with rolling pin or in food processor.

POUR milk into large bowl. Add pudding mix. Beat with wire whisk 2 minutes. Stir in whipped topping and half of the crushed cookies.

PLACE about 1 tablespoon crushed cookies into each cup. Fill cups about ¾ full with pudding mixture. Top with remaining crushed cookies.

REFRIGERATE until ready to serve. Garnish as desired.

Makes 8 to 10 servings

Sand Cups: Substitute 1 package (12 ounces) vanilla wafer cookies for chocolate sandwich cookies and JELL-O Vanilla Flavor Instant Pudding & Pie Filling for JELL-O Chocolate Flavor Instant Pudding & Pie Filling.

Dirt Cups and Sand Cups

Marshmallow Creme Cups

Prep: 5 minutes

1 jar (7½ ounces)
   marshmallow creme
1 tub (8 ounces) COOL
   WHIP Whipped
   Topping

1 package (12.5 ounces)
   chocolate-covered
   graham crackers,
   coarsely chopped

REMOVE lid from marshmallow creme. Microwave marshmallow creme on MEDIUM for 40 seconds. Spoon into large bowl. Gently stir in whipped topping until well mixed.

STIR in crumbled cookies. Spoon into 8 to 10 dessert cups. Serve immediately or refrigerate.   *Makes 8 to 10 servings*

COOL WHIP® "Trail" Mix

Prep: 1 minute

2 cups BAKER'S Semi-
   Sweet Real Chocolate
   Chips
1 cup peanuts

1 cup pretzel nuggets
1 tub (8 ounces) COOL
   WHIP Whipped
   Topping, thawed

MIX chocolate chips, peanuts and pretzels into whipped topping until well mixed. Spoon into 8 dessert cups. Serve immediately or refrigerate.   *Makes 8 servings*

Rocky Road Cups

Prep: 1 minute

1 cup peanuts
1 cup BAKER'S Semi-
   Sweet Real Chocolate
   Chips

1 cup miniature
   marshmallows
1 tub (8 ounces) COOL
   WHIP Whipped
   Topping, thawed

STIR peanuts, chocolate chips and marshmallows into whipped topping. Spoon into 8 dessert dishes or cups.

SERVE immediately or refrigerate 1 hour.   *Makes 8 servings*

Butter Pecan Parfaits

Prep: 5 minutes

1 tub (8 ounces) COOL WHIP Whipped Topping, thawed
½ cup chopped pecans
2 tablespoons maple-flavored syrup

1 cup coarsely crushed pecan shortbread cookies
½ cup KRAFT Butterscotch Topping

STIR whipped topping, pecans and syrup in medium bowl.

LAYER whipped topping mixture alternately with crushed cookies and butterscotch topping into 4 dessert glasses. Serve immediately or refrigerate 1 hour.   *Makes 4 servings*

Caramel Dip

Prep: 5 minutes

1 tub (8 ounces) COOL WHIP Whipped Topping, thawed
¾ cup KRAFT Caramel-Flavored Dessert Topping

Assorted cut-up fruits (such as apples, pears and bananas)
Assorted cookies

GENTLY stir whipped topping and caramel topping in large bowl.

SERVE with fruit and cookies.   *Makes about 3 cups*

Cool Bananas

Prep: 5 minutes

1 tub (8 ounces) COOL
  WHIP Whipped
  Topping, thawed
3 cups sliced bananas
  (about 3 large
  bananas)

KRAFT Chocolate-
  Flavored Dessert
  Topping

MIX whipped topping and banana slices in large bowl.

DIVIDE mixture into dessert dishes. Drizzle with chocolate topping. Serve immediately.   *Makes 10 servings*

Piña Colada Cream

Prep: 15 minutes

1 can (8 ounces) crushed
  pineapple in juice
1 cup cold milk
¼ teaspoon rum extract
  (optional)
1 package (4-serving size)
  JELL-O Vanilla Flavor
  Instant Pudding & Pie
  Filling

1 tub (8 ounces) COOL
  WHIP Whipped
  Topping, thawed
1 cup BAKER'S ANGEL
  FLAKE Coconut

DRAIN pineapple, reserving juice.

POUR pineapple juice, milk and rum extract in large bowl. Add pudding mix. Beat with wire whisk 1 to 2 minutes. Let stand 5 minutes. Gently stir in 2 cups whipped topping, coconut and drained pineapple. Spoon into individual dessert dishes or serving bowl. Garnish with remaining whipped topping. Serve immediately.   *Makes 4 servings*

Cool Bananas

MAKE EVERY DAY SPECIAL

There are many reasons and seasons for celebration, but the most important are those little things that happen every day. Treat yourself to a slice of decadent Peachy Berry Dessert after a hard day's work, or spoil the entire family with a scrumptious Toffee Bar Dessert. With COOL WHIP, every day is a celebration.

Peachy Berry Dessert (page 52)

50

Peachy Berry Dessert

Wow all your family and friends with this effortless dessert. Piled high with mouthwatering juicy peaches and fresh blueberries, nobody will be able to resist seconds.

Prep: 15 minutes

½ cup plus 1 tablespoon sugar
½ teaspoon ground cinnamon
½ package (15 ounces) refrigerated pie crust
1 tablespoon butter or margarine, melted
2 cans (15 ounces each) peach slices in juice

2 packages (8 ounces each) PHILADELPHIA Cream Cheese, softened
1 tub (12 ounces) COOL WHIP Whipped Topping, thawed
½ cup blueberries

HEAT oven to 400°F.

STIR 1 tablespoon sugar and cinnamon together in small bowl. Unfold crust; cut into 10 to 12 wedges. Place pastry wedges on cookie sheet, ½ inch apart. Brush with melted butter and sprinkle with sugar mixture. Bake 8 to 10 minutes or until lightly browned. Remove to wire rack; cool.

DRAIN peaches reserving ½ cup juice. Beat cream cheese and remaining ½ cup sugar in large bowl with wire whisk until smooth. Gradually beat in reserved juice. Fold in 4½ cups whipped topping. Spoon into shallow bowl. Top with remaining whipped topping, peaches and blueberries.

ARRANGE pastry wedges in pinwheel fashion on top.

Makes 10 to 12 servings

Variation: 3 cups fresh sliced peaches and ½ cup peach nectar may be substituted for canned peaches.

Café Mocha Shortcakes

Prep: 15 minutes

1 package (12 ounces)
    frozen pound cake,
    thawed, cut into
    8 slices
3 tablespoons butter <u>or</u>
    margarine, melted
5 tablespoons freshly
    brewed coffee
1 tablespoon sugar

1¼ teaspoons ground
    cinnamon
1 cup KRAFT Chocolate
    Flavored Dessert
    Topping
1 tub (8 ounces) COOL
    WHIP Whipped
    Topping, thawed

HEAT oven to 400°F.

PLACE cake slices on baking sheet. Stir butter, 2 tablespoons coffee, sugar and ¼ teaspoon cinnamon in small bowl. Brush evenly over cake slices. Bake 8 minutes or until lightly browned.

MIX chocolate topping, remaining coffee and cinnamon. Just before serving, place one cake slice on each of 8 dessert dishes. Top evenly with whipped topping. Drizzle with chocolate mixture.

Makes 8 servings

COOL WHIP®STERS

Prep: 5 minutes

1 tub (8 ounces) COOL
    WHIP Whipped
    Topping, thawed

2 cups cookie crumbs
    (chocolate sandwich,
    peanut butter, graham
    cracker <u>or</u> other
    variety)

STIR whipped topping and cookie crumbs in large bowl until blended. Scoop into 1-inch balls.

FREEZE 3 hours or overnight.

Makes about 2 dozen COOL WHIP®STERS

Toffee Bar Dessert

When the decadent crust of this dessert is combined with rich butterscotch pudding, the results are divine!

Prep: 20 minutes

1 cup flour
1 cup toffee bits
½ cup pecans, toasted, finely chopped
½ cup (1 stick) butter or margarine, melted
¼ cup sugar
2 cups cold milk

2 packages (4 serving size each) JELL-O Butterscotch Flavor Instant Pudding & Pie Filling
1 tub (8 ounces) COOL WHIP Whipped Topping, thawed

HEAT oven to 400°F.

MIX flour, ½ cup toffee bits, pecans, butter and sugar in large bowl until well mixed. Press firmly onto bottom of 13×9-inch pan. Bake 10 minutes or until lightly browned. Cool.

POUR milk into large bowl. Add pudding mixes. Beat with wire whisk 1 to 2 minutes or until well blended. Spread 1½ cups pudding onto bottom of crust.

GENTLY stir half of the whipped topping into remaining pudding. Spread over pudding in pan. Top with remaining whipped topping. Sprinkle with remaining toffee bits.

Cool Whip Fun Fact

Every second, consumers across America buy 6 tubs of COOL WHIP.

REFRIGERATE 3 hours or overnight.
Makes 15 servings

Toffee Bar Dessert

54

White Chocolate Berry Mousse Cake

Prep: 15 minutes

1¾ cups boiling water
1 package (8-serving size)
 or 2 packages
 (4-serving size each)
 JELL-O Brand
 Raspberry Flavor
 Gelatin Dessert
1 cup cold water
½ cup cold milk

1 package (4-serving size)
 JELL-O White
 Chocolate Flavor
 Instant Pudding & Pie
 Filling
1 tub (8 ounces) COOL
 WHIP Whipped
 Topping, thawed
9 to 10 sugar cookies

STIR boiling water into gelatin in large bowl 2 minutes or until completely dissolved. Stir in cold water. Pour 1½ cups gelatin into 9-inch round cake pan sprayed with no-stick cooking spray. Refrigerate 2 hours or until set but not firm (sticks to finger when touched lightly). Reserve remaining gelatin at room temperature.

POUR milk into reserved gelatin. Add pudding mix. Beat with wire whisk 2 minutes. Gently stir in 2 cups whipped topping. Spoon over gelatin in pan. Arrange cookies on pudding mixture to form crust. Cover with plastic wrap.

REFRIGERATE 4 hours or until firm. Unmold. Garnish with remaining whipped topping.   *Makes 8 to 10 servings*

Unmolding: Dip mold in warm water for about 15 seconds. Gently pull gelatin from around edges with moist fingers. Place moistened serving plate on top of mold. Invert mold and plate; holding mold and plate together, shake slightly to loosen. Gently remove mold and center gelatin on plate.

White Chocolate Berry Mousse Cake

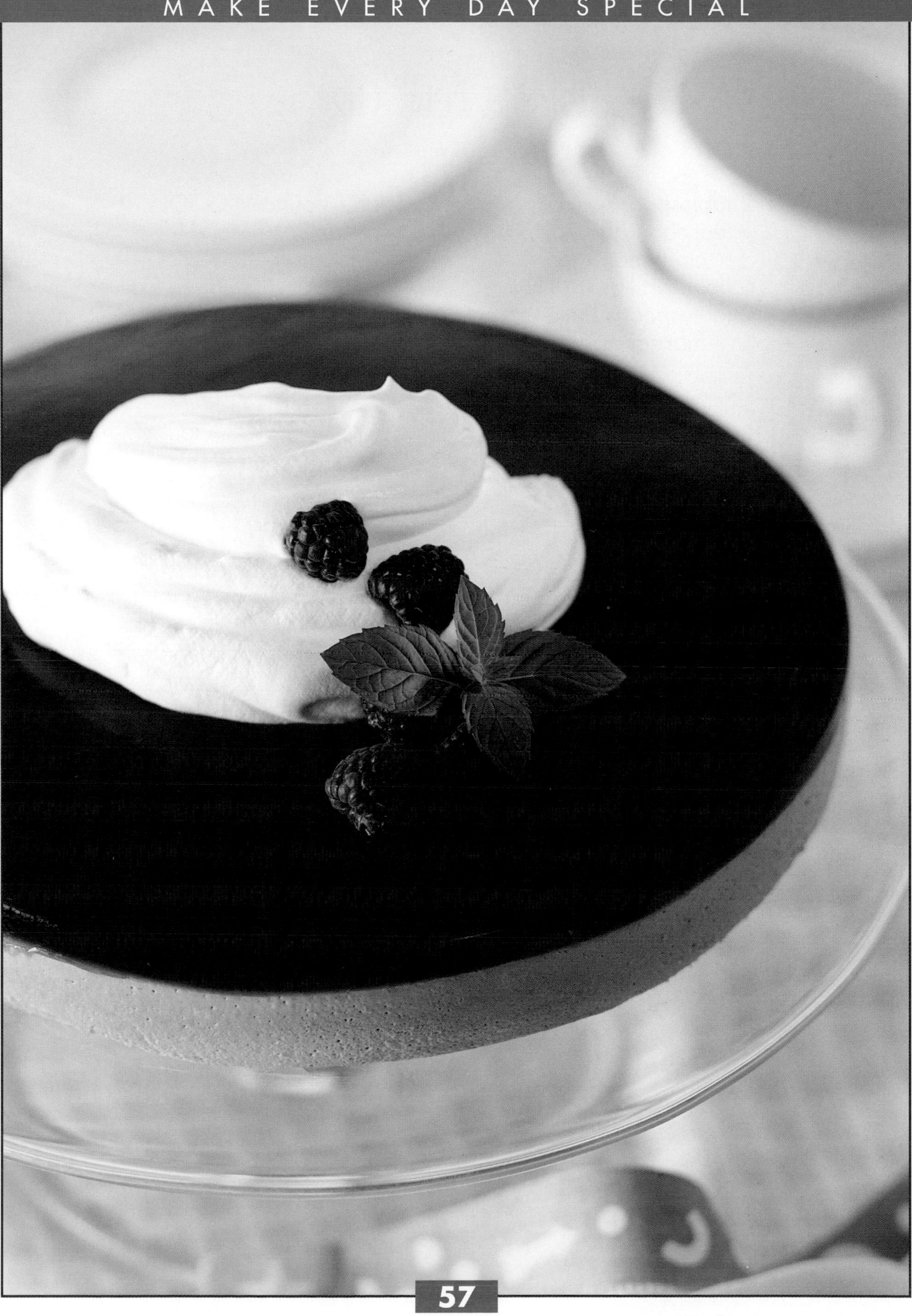

Tortilla Fruit Cups

Prep: 10 minutes

2 tablespoons sugar
1 teaspoon ground
    cinnamon
6 flour tortillas (8-inch)
2 tablespoons butter or
    margarine, melted

1 tub (8 ounces) COOL
    WHIP Whipped
    Topping, thawed
2 cups assorted cut-up fruit

HEAT oven to 400°F.

STIR sugar and cinnamon together in small bowl. Soften tortillas as directed on package. Brush 1 side of each tortilla with melted butter. Sprinkle evenly with sugar mixture.

GENTLY press tortillas into 6 (10-ounce) custard cups to form cups. Place cups in baking pan. Bake 15 minutes or until crisp. Remove from custard cups and cool on wire rack.

FILL tortilla cups with whipped topping and fruit.

Makes 6 servings

Watergate Salad

Prep: 10 minutes

1 package (4-serving size)
    JELL-O Pistachio
    Flavor Instant Pudding
    & Pie Filling
1 can (20 ounces) crushed
    pineapple in juice

1 cup miniature
    marshmallows
½ cup chopped nuts
2 cups thawed COOL
    WHIP Whipped
    Topping

STIR pudding mix, pineapple with juice, marshmallows and nuts in large bowl until well blended. Gently stir in whipped topping.

REFRIGERATE 1 hour or until ready to serve. Garnish with additional whipped topping and sliced strawberries, if desired.

Makes 8 servings

Tortilla Fruit Cups

Spiced Apple Berry Cups

Prep: 10 minutes

1 cup boiling water
1 package (4-serving size)
    JELL-O Brand
    Strawberry Flavor
    Gelatin Dessert
½ cup cold water

1 cup cinnamon-flavored
    applesauce
1 tub (8 ounces) COOL
    WHIP Whipped
    Topping, thawed

STIR boiling water into gelatin in large bowl 2 minutes or until completely dissolved. Stir in cold water and applesauce.

REMOVE 1½ cups gelatin. Refrigerate until consistency of thick syrup. Reserve remaining gelatin at room temperature. Stir 2¾ cups whipped topping into chilled gelatin. Spoon into 6 dessert glasses. Refrigerate 1 hour or until firm.

TOP with reserved gelatin. Refrigerate 2 hours or until firm. Garnish with remaining whipped topping.

Makes 6 servings

Lemon Ginger Squares

Prep: 15 minutes

2¼ cups gingersnap cookie
    crumbs
¼ cup sugar
⅓ cup butter <u>or</u> margarine,
    melted
⅔ cup boiling water
1 package (4-serving size)
    Lemon Flavor JELL-O
    Brand Gelatin

½ cup cold water
    Ice cubes
1 tub (12 ounces) COOL
    WHIP Whipped
    Topping, thawed

MIX 2 cups cookie crumbs, sugar and butter with fork in 13×9-inch baking pan until crumbs are well moistened. Press firmly onto bottom of pan. Refrigerate until ready to fill.

STIR boiling water into gelatin in large bowl 2 minutes until completely dissolved. Mix cold water and ice cubes to make 1¼ cups. Add to gelatin, stirring until slightly thickened (consistency of unbeaten egg whites). Remove any remaining ice. Stir in 3½ cups whipped topping with wire whisk until smooth. Pour over crust.

REFRIGERATE 3 hours or until firm. Just before serving, spread remaining whipped topping over gelatin mixture. Sprinkle with remaining cookie crumbs. Cut into squares. Garnish as desired.

Makes 15 to 18 servings

Easy Eclair Dessert

Prep: 20 minutes

27 whole graham crackers
3 cups cold milk
2 packages (4-serving size each) JELL-O Vanilla Flavor Instant Pudding & Pie Filling

1 tub (8 ounces) COOL WHIP Whipped Topping, thawed
1 can (16 ounces) chocolate fudge frosting

ARRANGE 9 crackers in bottom of 13×9-inch pan, cutting crackers to fit, if necessary.

POUR milk into large bowl. Add pudding mixes. Beat with wire whisk 1 minute. Gently stir in whipped topping. Spread half of the pudding mixture over crackers in pan. Place 9 of the remaining crackers over pudding. Top with remaining pudding mixture and crackers.

REMOVE lid and foil from frosting. Microwave frosting in container on HIGH 1 minute. Pour evenly over crackers.

REFRIGERATE 4 hours or overnight. Garnish as desired.

Makes 15 servings

Carrot Cake with Easy Cream Cheese Frosting

Prep: 20 minutes

1 package (2-layer size) carrot cake mix
1 package (8 ounces) PHILADELPHIA Cream Cheese, softened
⅓ cup granulated <u>or</u> powdered sugar
¼ cup cold milk
1 tub (8 ounces) COOL WHIP Whipped Topping, thawed

PREPARE cake mix as directed on package for 13×9-inch pan. Cool completely.

BEAT cream cheese, sugar and milk in medium bowl with wire whisk until smooth. Gently stir in whipped topping. Spread over top of cake.

REFRIGERATE until ready to serve. Garnish as desired.

Makes 10 servings

Note: Substitute your favorite carrot cake recipe for carrot cake mix.

KRAFT
Cool Whip
Fun Fact
In 1996, Fat Free COOL WHIP became the newest addition to the COOL WHIP family.

Carrot Cake with Easy Cream Cheese Frosting

COOL SENSATIONS

After a day of basking in the sun, beat the heat with a slice of refreshing Lemonade Stand Pie or rich and chilly Peanut Butter Snacking Cups. These cool treats and many more are the perfect way to add a splash of splendor to the dog days of summer. With COOL WHIP, it's easy to cool off!

Lemonade Stand Pie (page 66)

Lemonade Stand Pie

Prep: 10 minutes

1 can (6 ounces) frozen lemonade <u>or</u> pink lemonade concentrate, partially thawed

1 pint (2 cups) vanilla ice cream, softened

1 tub (8 ounces) COOL WHIP Whipped Topping, thawed

1 prepared graham cracker crumb crust (6 ounces <u>or</u> 9 inches)

BEAT lemonade concentrate in large bowl with electric mixer on low speed about 30 seconds. Spoon in ice cream; beat until well blended. Gently stir in whipped topping until smooth. Freeze, if necessary, until mixture will mound. Spoon into crust.

FREEZE 4 hours or overnight. Let stand at room temperature 15 minutes or until pie can be cut easily. Garnish with additional whipped topping, lemon slices and fresh mint leaves, if desired. *Makes 8 servings*

Cookie-Wiches

Prep: 15 minutes

1 tub (8 ounces) COOL WHIP Whipped Topping, thawed

24 assorted cookies

Suggested Garnishes: Sprinkles, finely crushed cookies, chocolate chips, chopped nuts, toasted coconut <u>or</u> assorted candies.

SPREAD whipped topping about ¾ inch thick on half of the cookies. Press remaining cookies lightly on top to make sandwiches. Roll or lightly press edges in garnish.

FREEZE 4 hours or overnight. Wrap individually and store in freezer up to 2 weeks. *Makes 12 servings*

Strawberry Shortcut

Prep: 10 minutes

1 package (12 ounces)
   pound cake, cut into
   14 slices
3 cups strawberries, sliced,
   sweetened

1 tub (8 ounces) COOL
   WHIP Whipped
   Topping, thawed

PLACE 7 cake slices on individual dessert plates.

SPOON about 3 tablespoons strawberries over each cake slice.
Top each with ¼ cup whipped topping. Repeat layers, ending
with a dollop of whipped topping. Garnish as desired. Serve
immediately.   *Makes 7 servings*

Frozen Peanut Butter Pie

Prep: 10 minutes

½ cup creamy peanut
   butter
1 cup cold milk
1 package (4-serving size)
   JELL-O Vanilla Flavor
   Instant Pudding & Pie
   Filling
1 tub (8 ounces) COOL
   WHIP Whipped
   Topping, thawed

1 prepared chocolate
   flavor crumb crust
   (6 ounces or 9 inches)
1 cup chopped peanut
   butter cookies
   (optional)
1 square BAKER'S Semi-
   Sweet Baking
   Chocolate, melted

BEAT peanut butter and milk in large bowl with wire whisk until
blended. Add pudding mix. Beat with wire whisk until smooth.
Stir in half of the whipped topping. Spoon half of the pudding
mixture into crust; top with cookies. Spoon remaining pudding
mixture over cookies.

FREEZE 3 hours or overnight. Drizzle with chocolate. Garnish
with remaining whipped topping.   *Makes 8 servings*

COOL WHIP® Flag Cake

Prep: 15 minutes

2 pints strawberries
1 package (12 ounces)
   frozen pound cake,
   thawed, cut into
   10 slices

1⅓ cups blueberries
1 tub (12 ounces) COOL
   WHIP Whipped
   Topping, thawed

SLICE 1 cup strawberries; set aside. Halve remaining strawberries; set aside.

LINE bottom of 12×8-inch baking dish with cake slices. Top with 1 cup sliced strawberries, 1 cup blueberries and whipped topping.

PLACE strawberry halves and remaining blueberries on whipped topping to create a flag design.

REFRIGERATE until ready to serve.   *Makes 15 servings*

All-American Sundae

COOL WHIP and ice cream go hand-in-hand. Choose your favorite ice cream to create the perfect flavor combination.

Prep: 5 minutes

1 slice pound cake
1 scoop vanilla ice cream,
   or any flavor
   KRAFT Strawberry
   Flavored Dessert
   Topping

Thawed COOL WHIP
   Whipped Topping
Fruit for garnish

TOP pound cake with ice cream, strawberry topping and whipped topping. Garnish with fruit.   *Makes 1 serving*

Top to bottom: COOL WHIP® Flag Cake and All-American Sundae

68

Fruit Salsa Parfaits

Prep: 5 minutes

1 can (15 ounces) peach slices in juice
1 can (8 ounces) pineapple chunks in juice
2 kiwi, peeled, chopped
1 cup strawberries, chopped
3 tablespoons packed brown sugar
½ teaspoon ground ginger
¼ teaspoon ground allspice
1 tub (8 ounces) COOL WHIP Whipped Topping, thawed

DRAIN peaches and pineapple, reserving juices. Chop peaches and pineapple.

STIR peaches, pineapple, kiwi, strawberries, 1 tablespoon brown sugar, ginger and allspice in medium bowl; set aside. Mix reserved juices and remaining brown sugar in large bowl. Gently stir in whipped topping.

LAYER fruit alternately with whipped topping mixture in 6 dessert dishes.
Makes 6 servings

COOL WHIP® Cookie Bars

Prep: 10 minutes

1 cup crushed chocolate sandwich cookies
3 tablespoons butter or margarine, melted
1 tub (8 ounces) COOL WHIP Whipped Topping, thawed
2 cups chopped chocolate sandwich cookies

MIX crushed cookies and butter in small bowl. Press onto bottom of foil-lined 8-inch square pan. Mix whipped topping and chopped cookies in large bowl. Spread over crust.

FREEZE 4 hours or overnight. Cut into squares. Garnish as desired.
Makes 9 servings

Fruit Salsa Parfaits

Peanut Butter Snacking Cups

Prep: 10 minutes

¾ cup graham cracker
    crumbs
3 tablespoons butter or
    margarine, melted
3½ cups (8 ounces) COOL
    WHIP Whipped
    Topping, thawed
1 cup milk

½ cup chunky peanut
    butter
1 package (4-serving size)
    JELL-O Vanilla Flavor
    Instant Pudding & Pie
    Filling
¼ cup strawberry
    preserves

LINE 12 muffin cups with paper baking cups. Mix graham cracker crumbs and butter in small bowl. Press about 1 tablespoon crumb mixture into each cup. Top each with about 1 tablespoon whipped topping.

GRADUALLY add milk to peanut butter in medium bowl; blend until smooth. Add pudding mix. Beat 1 to 2 minutes until blended. Fold in remaining whipped topping. Spoon into cups. Top each with 1 teaspoon preserves.

FREEZE 4 hours or overnight. Peel off paper before serving.

Makes 12 servings

COOL 'N EASY® Pie

Prep: 20 minutes

⅔ cup boiling water
1 package (4-serving size)
    JELL-O Brand Gelatin
    Dessert, any flavor
½ cup cold water
    Ice cubes

1 tub (8 ounces) COOL
    WHIP Whipped
    Topping, thawed
1 prepared graham
    cracker crust
    (6 ounces or 9 inches)
Assorted fruit (optional)

STIR boiling water into gelatin in large bowl at least 2 minutes or until completely dissolved. Mix cold water and ice to make 1¼ cups. Add to gelatin, stirring until slightly thickened. Remove remaining ice.

STIR in 2½ cups whipped topping with wire whisk until smooth. Refrigerate 10 to 15 minutes or until mixture is very thick and will mound. Spoon into crust.

REFRIGERATE 4 hours or until set. Just before serving, garnish with remaining whipped topping and fruit.

Makes 8 servings

Frozen Yogurt Pie

Prep: 10 minutes

2 containers (8 ounces each) BREYERS Lowfat Yogurt, any fruit flavor
1 tub (8 ounces) COOL WHIP Whipped Topping, thawed

1 prepared graham cracker crumb crust (6 ounces <u>or</u> 9 inches)

GENTLY stir yogurt into whipped topping in large bowl until well blended. Spoon into crust.

FREEZE 4 hours or overnight. Let stand at room temperature 15 minutes or until pie can be cut easily. Garnish with additional whipped topping and fruit, if desired.

Makes 8 servings

Frozen Strawberry Yogurt Pie: Use BREYERS Strawberry Lowfat Yogurt and stir in 2 cups sweetened sliced <u>or</u> finely chopped strawberries.

Strawberry Margarita Pie

Prep: 10 minutes

1¼ cups crushed pretzels
¼ cup sugar
10 tablespoons butter <u>or</u> margarine, melted
1 can (14 ounces) sweetened condensed milk

2 cups strawberries, crushed or puréed
½ cup lime juice
1 tub (8 ounces) COOL WHIP Whipped Topping, thawed

MIX pretzels, sugar and butter in 9-inch pie plate. Press mixture onto bottom and up side of pie plate. Refrigerate until ready to fill.

MIX condensed milk, strawberries and lime juice in large bowl until well blended. Gently stir in whipped topping. Pour into prepared crust.

FREEZE 6 hours or overnight. Let stand at room temperature 15 minutes or until pie can be cut easily. Garnish with additional whipped topping, strawberries and lime peel, if desired.   *Makes 8 servings*

Helpful Hint: Dip pie plate into warm water, just to rim, for 30 seconds for easy serving.

Note: Two prepared graham cracker crumb crusts (6 ounces <u>or</u> 9 inches each) can be substituted for the homemade crust. Divide filling equally between the 2 pie crusts.

Lime Margarita Pie: Omit strawberries and lime juice; add one 12-ounce can lime juice concentrate; proceed as above.

Cool Whip Fun Fact — For 20 years, consumers have enjoyed COOL 'N EASY® Pie (p.72), a classic COOL WHIP dessert.

Strawberry Margarita Pie

Frozen Creamy Pudding Pops

Prep: 10 minutes

1½ cups cold milk
1 package (4-serving size) JELL-O Instant Pudding & Pie Filling, any flavor

2 cups thawed COOL WHIP Whipped Topping
Additions (see below)
9 (5-ounce) paper <u>or</u> plastic cups <u>or</u> popsicle molds

POUR milk into medium bowl. Add pudding mix. Beat with wire whisk 2 minutes. Gently stir in whipped topping. Stir in desired Additions. Spoon into cups. Insert wooden popsicle stick into each for handle.

FREEZE 5 hours or overnight. To remove pop from cup, place bottom of cup under running water for 15 seconds. Press firmly on bottom of cup to release pop. Do not twist or pull popsicle stick.   *Makes 9 pops*

ADDITIONS:

½ cup chopped cookies

½ cup chopped toffee candy

½ cup mashed banana

½ cup miniature marshmallows and ¼ cup each chopped peanuts and BAKER'S Semi-Sweet Real Chocolate Chips

SPECIAL ADDITIONS: Stir in ¼ cup GENERAL FOODS INTERNATIONAL COFFEES, any flavor, with pudding mix.

Ice Cream Shop Pie

Prep: 15 minutes

1½ cups cold milk, half-and-half <u>or</u> light cream
1 package (4-serving size) JELL-O Instant Pudding & Pie Filling, any flavor

1 tub (8 ounces) COOL WHIP Whipped Topping, thawed
1 prepared crumb crust (6 ounces <u>or</u> 9 inches)

POUR milk into large bowl. Add pudding mix. Beat with wire whisk 2 minutes. Gently stir in whipped topping. Spoon into crust.

FREEZE 4 hours or over night. Let stand at room temperature or in refrigerator 15 minutes or until pie can be cut easily. Garnish as desired.   *Makes 8 servings*

Cookies and Cream Pie: Use JELL-O Vanilla Flavor Instant Pudding & Pie Filling and chocolate crumb crust. Stir in 1 cup chopped chocolate sandwich cookies with whipped topping. Garnish with additional chocolate sandwich cookies, if desired.

Rocky Road Pie: Use JELL-O Chocolate Flavor Instant Pudding & Pie Filling and chocolate crumb crust. Stir in ⅓ cup <u>each</u> BAKER'S Semi-Sweet Real Chocolate Chips, miniature marshmallows and chopped nuts with whipped topping. Serve with chocolate sauce, if desired.

Peanut Butter Pie: Use JELL-O Vanilla Flavor Instant Pudding & Pie Filling and graham cracker crust. Reduce milk to 1 cup and add ½ cup peanut butter with pudding mix. Serve with chocolate sauce and chopped peanuts, if desired.

Raspberry Summer Sensation

Looking for a special dessert for a summer get-together? Look no further. This refreshing show-stopping treat is simple to make and the perfect finale to any meal.

Prep: 10 minutes

1 pint (2 cups) raspberry sorbet <u>or</u> sherbet, softened
1 cup cold milk
1 package (4-serving size) JELL-O Vanilla Flavor Instant Pudding & Pie Filling

1 tub (8 ounces) COOL WHIP Whipped Topping, thawed
Raspberries, strawberries and blueberries for garnish (optional)

LINE 8×4-inch loaf pan with foil. Spoon sorbet into pan; freeze 10 minutes.

POUR milk into large bowl. Add pudding mix. Beat with wire whisk 2 minutes. Stir in 3 cups whipped topping. Spread over sorbet in pan.

FREEZE 3 hours or overnight. Unmold onto plate; remove foil. Top with remaining whipped topping; garnish as desired.

Makes 10 servings

Cool Whip® KRAFT

Fun Fact

COOL WHIP built the world's largest COOL WHIP® Flag Cake (p.68) at the Statue of Liberty in 1997; over 3000 Cool Whip tubs were used.

Helpful Hint: Soften sorbet in microwave on MEDIUM 10 to 15 seconds.

Raspberry Summer Sensation

EASY INDULGENCES

Discover how decadent COOL WHIP treats can be. Dive into thick and rich Cappuccino Bars or relish the creamy texture of Truffle Treats. And better yet, you don't have to spend hours in the kitchen—it just tastes like you did. Shhh, let that be our little secret.

Cappuccino Bars (page 82)

Cappuccino Bars

One bite of this fabulous bar and you will be in heaven.
The rich coffee flavor topped off with creamy COOL WHIP
makes this an irresistible dessert.

Prep: 10 minutes

15 whole chocolate graham crackers, divided
2 packages (8 ounces each) PHILADELPHIA Cream Cheese, softened
3½ cups cold milk
3 packages (4-serving size each) JELL-O Chocolate Flavor Instant Pudding & Pie Filling

1 tablespoon MAXWELL HOUSE Instant Coffee
¼ teaspoon ground cinnamon
1 tub (8 ounces) COOL WHIP Whipped Topping, thawed
1 square BAKER'S Semi-Sweet Baking Chocolate, grated **or** 3 tablespoons chocolate sprinkles

ARRANGE half of the crackers in bottom of 13×9-inch pan, cutting crackers to fit, if necessary.

BEAT cream cheese in large bowl with electric mixer on low speed until smooth. Gradually beat in 1 cup milk. Add remaining milk, pudding mixes, instant coffee and cinnamon. Beat 1 to 2 minutes. (Mixture will be thick.) Gently stir in 2 cups whipped topping.

SPREAD half of the pudding mixture over crackers in pan. Arrange remaining crackers over pudding in pan. Top with remaining pudding mixture. Cover with remaining whipped topping. Sprinkle with grated chocolate.

FREEZE 3 hours or overnight. Cut into bars. Garnish as desired.

Makes 18 servings

Cannoli Parfaits

Prep: 10 minutes

1 container (15 ounces) ricotta cheese
⅓ cup powdered sugar
2 tablespoons orange juice
1 to 2 teaspoons grated orange peel
1½ teaspoons vanilla

1 tub (8 ounces) COOL WHIP Whipped Topping, thawed
½ cup dried mixed fruit
½ cup BAKER'S Semi-Sweet Real Chocolate Chips
1 cup vanilla wafer cookie crumbs

MIX cheese, sugar, orange juice, orange peel and vanilla in medium bowl. Gently stir in 2 cups whipped topping. Stir in mixed fruit and chocolate chips.

LAYER cookie crumbs, cheese mixture and remaining whipped topping alternately into 6 parfait glasses.

REFRIGERATE at least 1 hour or until ready to serve. Garnish as desired.

Makes 6 servings

COOL WHIP Fun Fact

COOL WHIP is America's favorite whipped topping. Almost 1 in 2 households buy COOL WHIP every year.

Black & White Bombe

Prep: 20 minutes

1 package (12 ounces)
   pound cake, cut into
   10 slices
2 cups milk
1 package (4-serving size)
   JELL-O Devil's Food
   Flavor Instant Pudding
   & Pie Filling
2 tubs (8 ounces each)
   COOL WHIP
   Whipped Topping,
   thawed

1 package (4-serving size)
   JELL-O White
   Chocolate Flavor
   Instant Pudding & Pie
   Filling
2 squares BAKER'S Semi-
   Sweet Baking
   Chocolate, melted
   (optional)

CUT cake slices in half to form triangles. Line 2-quart bowl with plastic wrap. Arrange cake triangles in bottom and up side of bowl, reserving 5 triangles for top.

POUR 1 cup milk into large bowl. Add devil's food pudding mix. Beat with wire whisk 1 minute. Gently stir in half of one tub of the whipped topping. Spoon into bowl over cake slices.

POUR remaining milk into large bowl; add white chocolate pudding mix. Beat with wire whisk 1 minute. Gently stir in half of one tub of the whipped topping. Spoon into bowl. Press remaining cake slices on top.

REFRIGERATE 4 hours or overnight. Invert mold onto plate. Remove plastic wrap. Frost with remaining tub whipped topping. Drizzle with chocolate, if desired.

Makes 10 servings

Black & White Bombe

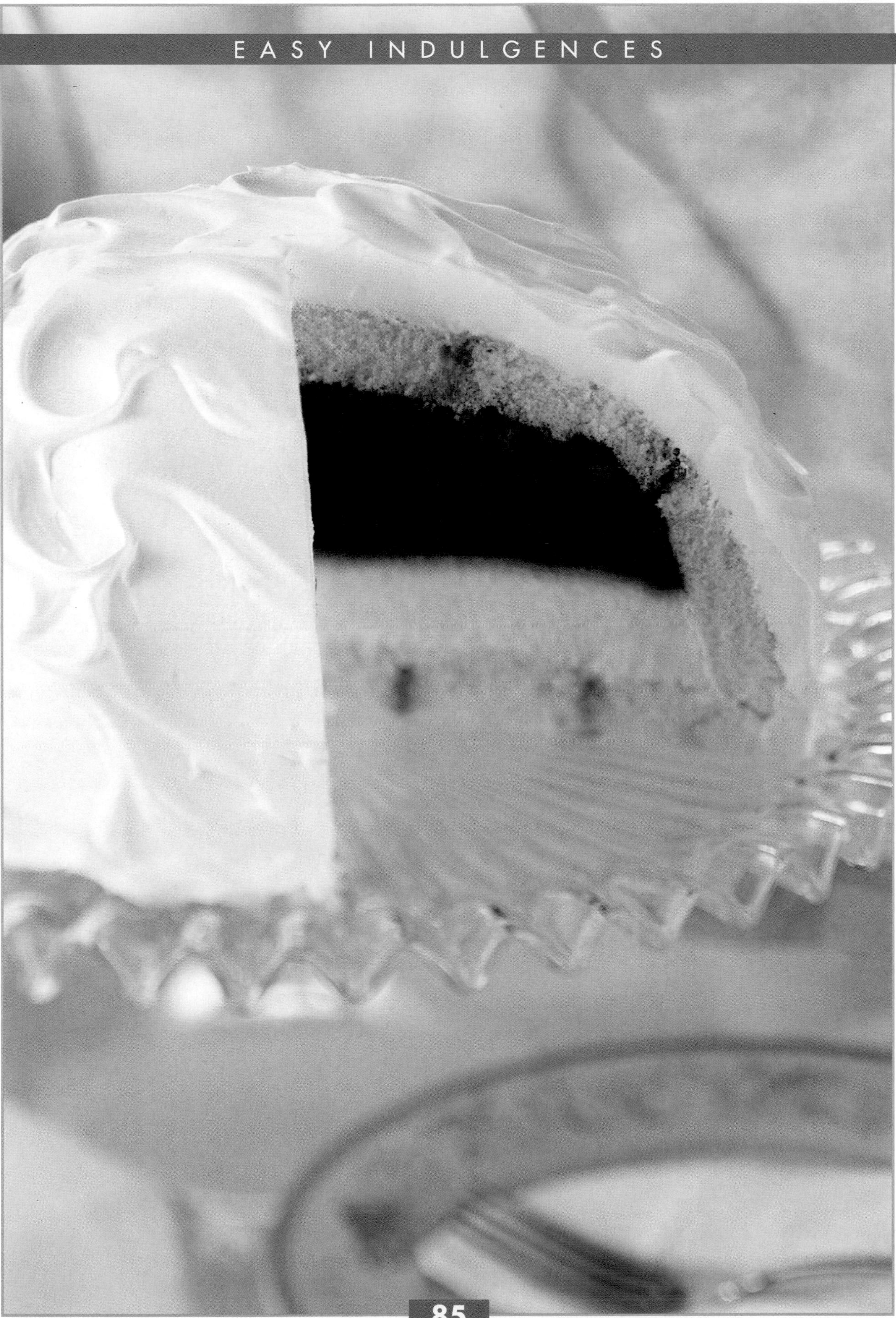

Truffle Treats

Terrific truffles are just moments away. With COOL WHIP all the richness of truffles can be yours without all the extra work.

Prep: 10 minutes

1 package (8 ounces) BAKER'S Semi-Sweet Baking Chocolate Squares
½ cup peanut butter
1 tub (8 ounces) COOL WHIP Extra Creamy Whipped Topping, thawed

Powdered sugar, chopped nuts, cocoa powder, chocolate sprinkles, grated BAKER'S Semi-Sweet Baking Chocolate Squares

MICROWAVE chocolate in microwavable bowl on HIGH 3 minutes or until chocolate is almost melted, stirring halfway through heating time. Stir until chocolate is completely melted.

MIX in peanut butter until smooth. Cool to room temperature. Gently stir in whipped topping. Refrigerate 1 hour.

ROLL mixture into 1-inch balls. Coat with desired toppings.

Makes 35 to 40 treats

Variation: Substitute 8 squares BAKER'S Premium White Baking Chocolate for Semi-Sweet Baking Chocolate.

Truffle Treats

Easy Celebration Ice Cream Cake

This year make that special holiday or birthday cake just the way you like it—with the tantalizing flavor of your favorite ice cream.

Prep: 15 minutes

10 chocolate wafer cookies
1 pint (2 cups) ice cream,
    any flavor, softened
1 jar (16 ounces)
    chocolate fudge sauce
3 packages (2.07 ounces
    each) chocolate-
    covered caramel
    peanut nougat bars,
    chopped

1 tub (8 ounces) COOL
    WHIP Whipped
    Topping, thawed

LINE 9-inch round cake pan with plastic wrap. Arrange cookies in bottom of pan. Spread ice cream over cookies. Reserve ½ cup fudge sauce. Pour remaining fudge sauce over ice cream.

MIX candy into whipped topping. Spread whipped topping mixture over fudge sauce in pan. Drizzle with reserved fudge sauce.

FREEZE 4 hours or overnight. Lift cake out of pan; peel off plastic wrap. Let stand 10 minutes. Top with additional candy, if desired.

Makes 10 servings

KRAFT
Cool Whip *Fun Fact*
The COOL WHIP brand name is recognized by 99% of Americans.

Easy Celebration Ice Cream Cake

Decadent Triple Layer Mud Pie

This luscious pie with its rich fudgy bottom layer, golden toasted pecans and smooth chocolate pudding is a chocoholic's dream. Top it off with eye-catching swirls of creamy COOL WHIP for the perfect decadent dessert.

Prep: 10 minutes

2 squares BAKER'S Semi-Sweet Baking Chocolate, melted
¼ cup sweetened condensed milk
1 prepared chocolate flavor crumb crust (6 ounces or 9 inches)
¾ cup chopped pecans, toasted

2 cups cold milk
2 packages (4-serving size each) JELL-O Chocolate Flavor Instant Pudding & Pie Filling
1 tub (8 ounces) COOL WHIP Whipped Topping, thawed

POUR chocolate and sweetened condensed milk into bowl; stir until smooth. Pour into crust. Press nuts evenly into chocolate in crust. Refrigerate 10 minutes.

POUR milk into large bowl. Add pudding mixes. Beat with wire whisk 1 minute. (Mixture will be thick.) Spoon 1½ cups pudding over pecans in crust.

STIR half of the whipped topping into remaining pudding. Spread over pudding in crust. Top with remaining whipped topping.

REFRIGERATE 3 hours. Garnish as desired.

Makes 8 servings

Decadent Triple Layer Mud Pie

Triple Layer Bars

Prep: 25 minutes

1 cup flour
1 cup finely chopped
    pecans
¼ cup sugar
½ cup (1 stick) butter or
    margarine, melted
1 package (8 ounces)
    PHILADELPHIA Cream
    Cheese, softened
¼ cup sugar
2 tablespoons milk
1 tub (8 ounces) COOL
    WHIP Whipped
    Topping, thawed

3½ cups cold milk
1 package (4-serving size)
    JELL-O Chocolate
    Flavor Instant Pudding
    & Pie Filling
1 package (4-serving size)
    JELL-O Vanilla Flavor
    Instant Pudding & Pie
    Filling
2 squares BAKER'S Semi-
    Sweet Baking
    Chocolate, grated
    (optional)

HEAT oven to 350°F.

MIX flour, pecans, ¼ cup sugar and butter until flour is moistened. Press onto bottom of 13×9-inch pan. Bake 20 minutes or until lightly browned; cool.

BEAT cream cheese, ¼ cup sugar and 2 tablespoons milk in large bowl with wire whisk until smooth. Gently stir in 1½ cups whipped topping. Spread over cooled crust.

POUR 1¾ cups cold milk into large bowl. Add chocolate pudding mix. Beat with wire whisk 1 minute. Gently stir in 1 cup whipped topping. Pour over cream cheese layer.

POUR remaining 1¾ cups milk into large bowl. Add vanilla pudding mix. Beat with wire whisk 1 minute. Gently stir in remaining whipped topping. Pour over chocolate pudding layer.

REFRIGERATE 4 hours or until set. Just before serving, garnish with grated chocolate.   *Makes 15 servings*

I'M WORRIED

By Michael Ian Black

Illustrated by Debbie Ridpath Ohi

SIMON & SCHUSTER BOOKS FOR YOUNG READERS

New York   London   Toronto   Sydney   New Delhi

I'm worried.

Why are you worried about the future?

Because what if something **BAD** happens?

Please tell me nothing bad will ever happen.

I wish I could, Potato, but I can't.

Because **nobody** knows what's going to happen.

WHY NOT???

Um, now I'M worried.

It's okay, you two.
Sometimes bad things happen.
Like, Potato, remember that time
you rolled off the table?

I was bruised for **weeks.**

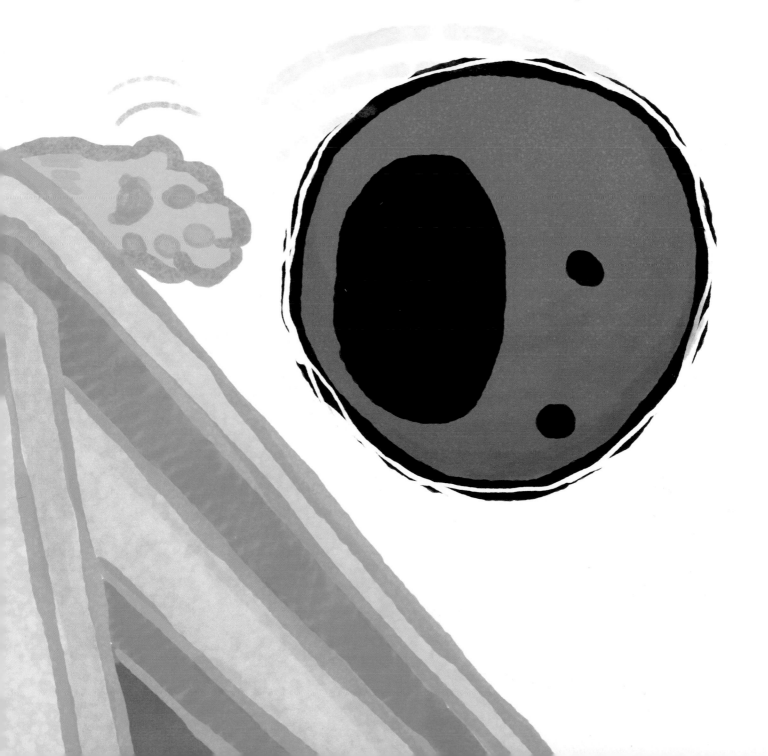

And, Flamingo, remember when

you got your beak stuck in the peanut butter jar?

Peanut butter is the worst.

And that time I fell off the monkey bars and broke my arm?

All of those things were bad at first . . .

I got a sticker at the
doctor's office and it was
scratch 'n' sniff!

Power to the Potato

I put bologna on my sandwich
and it was delicious!

You both doodled all over my cast and it looked **awesome!**

I'm going to wrap
myself in
Bubble Wrap,
just in case.

That way nothing bad
can happen again!

Guys . . .

See?

Worrying
doesn't help!

Hey, Flamingo.

Yeah?

Enjoying the now is **way** better than worrying about the future!

(But peanut butter
is still the worst.)

worried worried worried worried worried worried worried worried worried worried worried worried worried worried

worried worried worried worried worried worried worried worried worried wo

worried worried worried worried worried worried worried wo

worried worried worried worried worried worried

worried worried worried worried wo

Worried Worried Worried

ORRIED WORRIED WOR

WORRIED

WORRIED WORRIE

WOR